Understanding Money

Money through History

Lori McManus

www.raintreepublishers.co.uk
Visit our website to find out
more information about
Raintree books.

To order:
☎ Phone 0845 6044371
📄 Fax +44 (0) 1865 312263
💻 Email myorders@raintreepublishers.co.uk

Customers from outside the UK please telephone +44 1865 312262

Raintree is an imprint of Capstone Global Library Limited,
a company incorporated in England and Wales having its
registered office at 7 Pilgrim Street, London, EC4V 6LB –
Registered company number: 6695582

Text © Capstone Global Library Limited 2011
First published in hardback in 2011
Paperback edition first published in 2012
The moral rights of the proprietor have been asserted.

Edited by Megan Cotugno
Designed by Ryan Frieson
Original illustrations © Capstone Global Library, Ltd.
Illustrated by Planman Technologies
Picture research by Mica Brancic
Originated by Capstone Global Library, Ltd.
Printed and bound in China by Leo Paper Products Ltd.

ISBN 978 1 4062 2168 8 (hardback)
15 14 13 12 11
10 9 8 7 6 5 4 3 2 1

ISBN 978 1 4062 2175 6 (paperback)
16 15 14 13 12
10 9 8 7 6 5 4 3 2 1

British Library Cataloguing in Publication Data
McManus, Lori.
  Money through history. -- (Understanding money)
  1. Money--History--Juvenile literature.
  I. Title II. Series
  332.4'9-dc22

Acknowledgements

The author and publishers are grateful to the following for
permission to reproduce copyright material:

Art Archive p. 7 (Government Palace Tlaxcala Mexico/Dagli
Orti); British Museum pp. 12, 14, 1516, 18, 25, 26 (© The
Trustees of the British Museum); Corbis pp. 17 (© The Gallery
Collection), 19 (© Hulton-Deutsch Collection), 21 (© Michael
Nicholson), 41 (image100); Getty Images pp. 4 (Jamie Grill),
10 (Karl Newedel), 20, 27 (Hulton Archive), 34 (Bloomberg/
Contributor); iStockphoto.com pp. 13 (© mrundbaken), 43 (©
leezsnow), 22 (© Buretsu), 29 (© Khoroshkov), 31 (© elgol),
32 (© enriquerodben), 35 (© biffspandex), 37 (© Liveshot);
Shutterstock pp. 5 (© Lim Yong Hian), 8 (© nito), 11 (©
africa924)

Cover photograph of Roman silver Antoninianus coin,
showing Emperor Philip I, Rome AD 245-247, reproduced
with permission of Shutterstock (© Keith Wheatley).

We would like to thank Michael Miller for his invaluable help
in the preparation of this book.

Every effort has been made to contact copyright holders of
any material reproduced in this book. Any omissions will
be rectified in subsequent printings if notice is given to the
publisher.

All the Internet addresses (URLs) given in this book were valid
at the time of going to press. However, due to the dynamic
nature of the Internet, some addresses may have changed, or
sites may have changed or ceased to exist since publication.
While the author and Publishers regret any inconvenience this
may cause readers, no responsibility for any such changes can
be accepted by either the author or the Publishers.

Contents

You can find the answers to the Solve it! questions on page 45.

Some words are shown in bold, **like this**. You can find out what they mean by looking in the glossary on page 46.

What is money?

Money comes in different forms. Some people use coins and paper banknotes as money. Others use plastic cards. Money can even exist as a file on a computer. Long ago, people used shells, feathers, stones, and even cows as money. How can all of these different objects be money?

The word "money" describes anything that can be used to pay for goods and services. Goods are things that are made, sold, and purchased. Services are things that one person pays another person to do.

If a coin can buy food and clothes, that coin is money. If a plastic card pays for food, that card is money. The government of a country decides what counts as money. For example, in Japan paper banknotes and coins called yen are used as money.

Today, many people use plastic credit cards as money.

Changing money

Money has changed through history. In ancient days, money did not even exist. Instead, people traded goods and services for other goods and services. Over time, communities developed money using objects, metals, and paper. Often, a country's money is decorated with pictures of its leaders or meaningful **symbols**. The symbols stand for ideas like freedom, courage, or strength.

Japanese yen can purchase goods and services in the country of Japan, but not in other countries. The man pictured on this 1000 yen bill was a famous Japanese doctor.

Plastic money

In 1988, Australia became the first country to produce a complete set of plastic banknotes. These banknotes or **bills**, last four times longer than paper money. They are almost impossible to tear. Now, more than 20 other countries have switched to plastic banknotes, including Mexico, Brazil, Romania, and New Zealand.

How did trade develop in ancient times?

In early societies, people did not need money. Before 10,000 BC, most people provided food for their families by hunting, fishing, and gathering nuts and berries. They made clothing from animal skins. These ancient people lived in caves or built homes from mud, grasses, and branches. They worked together in family groups to meet their needs.

The beginning of trade

As the human population grew larger, more food was needed. Family groups moved from place to place to follow herds of animals or find new places to fish. During their travels, they met unfamiliar groups of people. In time, these groups began to trade with one another. Each group could get the items they needed or wanted by giving away some of their extra supplies. One group might offer deer meat in exchange for fish. Animal skins might be traded for fruit.

Fair exchange

Any object could be traded as long as the two people agreed that it was a fair exchange. For example, one animal skin might be traded for ten fish. Twenty pretty shells might be exchanged for five colourful feathers. The exchange of goods without using money is called **barter**.

Solve it!

Possible trade agreement in ancient times

1 animal skin = 10 fish
1 fish = 5 feathers

Based on the trading agreement listed above, how many feathers could a trader get for two animal skins?

Family groups eventually began trading goods with other ancient people. Often, the trading involved food.

7

The development of farming

Over many years, people's way of life began to change. Family groups started to settle and develop new ways of getting food. Around 8000 BC, people learned how to grow crops and raise animals on farms. Families produced enough food for themselves with a little left over for trade.

Special skills

Some people stopped farming and began to develop special skills. By 6000 BC, potters made clay jars for storing and cooking food. Other people became skilled at making farm tools, building boats, or grinding grain into flour. By specializing in one skill, people made or grew more goods than they could use. They also began to live closer together in towns and villages.

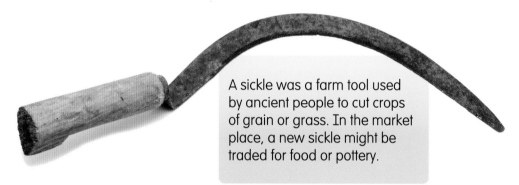

A sickle was a farm tool used by ancient people to cut crops of grain or grass. In the market place, a new sickle might be traded for food or pottery.

Trading in the market place

On arranged days, people brought their **surplus** (extra) goods to the marketplace in the village. Here, a goat might be exchanged for tools. Several loaves of bread could be traded for a bead necklace. Even work could be exchanged for goods. A miller might grind grain in exchange for a woven basket. All buying and selling was done through barter.

How did crops grow in the desert?

The Nile, Tigris, and Euphrates rivers flooded each year, making it possible to grow crops in areas that did not receive much rainfall.

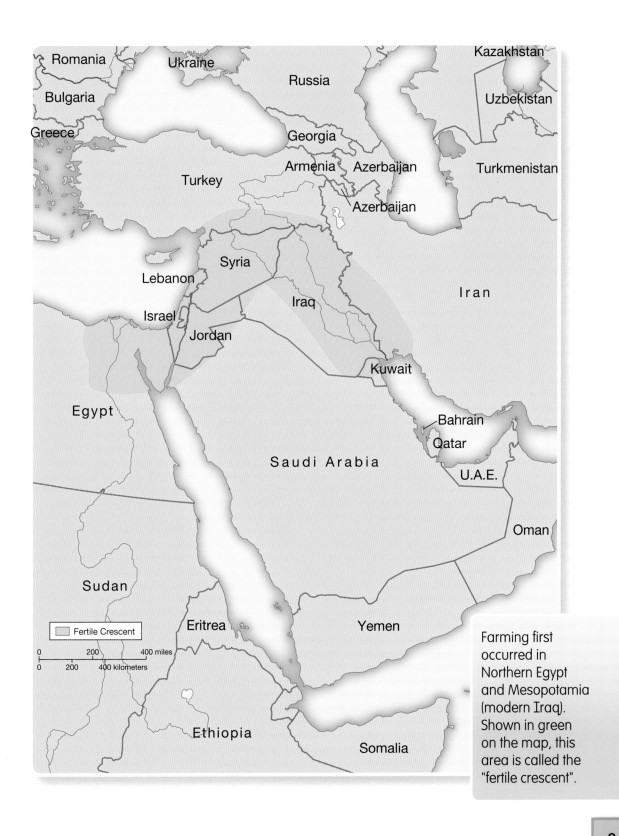

Romania
Ukraine
Russia
Kazakhstan
Bulgaria
Uzbekistan
Greece
Georgia
Armenia   Azerbaijan
Turkmenistan
Turkey
Azerbaijan
Syria
Lebanon
Iraq
Iran
Israel
Jordan
Kuwait
Egypt
Bahrain
Qatar
Saudi Arabia
U.A.E.
Oman
Sudan
Eritrea
Yemen
Fertile Crescent
0   200   400 miles
0   200   400 kilometers
Ethiopia
Somalia

Farming first
occurred in
Northern Egypt
and Mesopotamia
(modern Iraq).
Shown in green
on the map, this
area is called the
"fertile crescent".

How did money begin?

People started using objects as money when **bartering** became too complicated. What if the carpenter did not need the two rugs being offered for his table? Who would decide how much wheat is equal in value to a boat? To make trading easier, people in different parts of the world began to use objects as **currency**, or money.

What money came first?

Around 6000 BC, animals and food became the first objects used as money. People in a particular area decided the worth of an animal such as a cow or goat. The animal could then be used to buy goods. Other types of early money included barley (ancient Sumer, now the **Middle East**), almonds (India), and salt (China and the Mediterranean region).

Salt is essential for life. It was also valuable in ancient societies because it added flavour to food and could keep meat from spoiling.

Problems with food and animals

The first objects used as money did not always last well over time. Salt could be ruined in the rain. Grains like barley or wheat often rotted and lost their value. Cows lasted well but could not be divided to make small purchases. As time passed, traders started using money that could survive bad weather. They also looked for objects that could be carried easily during long journeys.

Have a cow!

Historians believe that cows were the first form of money. Cows started being used as money between 8000–6000 BC. They were valuable because they provided food and clothing. In parts of Africa, cows were used as money until the mid-1900s!

Metal money

Ancient people realized metal could be a long-lasting form of money. By 1850 BC, people used lumps of gold, silver, and bronze to buy goods. These lumps of metal were called **ingots**. The Sumerians in ancient Mesopotamia (modern Iraq) were the first people to use ingots. As they travelled, they spread the idea of using metal as money. Ingots were shaped as bars, rings, rods, and loops.

What is an ingot worth?

Since ingots varied in size and shape, their value depended on their weight. The heavier the ingot, the more it was worth. **Merchants** receiving ingots weighed them carefully before accepting them as payment.

Ingots were the first form of metal money.

Problems with ingots

Merchants could not tell by appearance alone if the gold or silver in an ingot had been mixed with less valuable metals. This made it difficult to know the true value of the money. The invention of stamped metal coins solved this problem.

Code of Hammurabi

King Hammurabi ruled the Babylonian Empire from 1792–1750 BC. He created the first set of written laws (the Code of Hammurabi) to keep order in his kingdom. The Code explained how people should use money and trade fairly.

Sea shells as money

Have you ever collected sea shells near the ocean? By around 1400 BC, sea shells called cowries (shown above) were used as money in the Shang Dynasty of Ancient China. Later, people in India and Africa also used cowrie shells as money. Other long-lasting forms of ancient money included beads, stones, tools, and even animal teeth!

Who invented coins?

Around 640 BC, the government of Lydia (modern Turkey) began to make coins to use as money. Each coin was stamped with a **seal** that stated its weight and the purity of the metal. The coins were also stamped with the heads of a lion and a bull facing each other. The lion's head was the mark of the king of Lydia. The seal guaranteed that the coin was worth the amount stamped on it.

These ancient Lydian **staters** were the world's first coins. They were made from a mixture of silver and gold, called electrum.

The spread of coins

Coins were easy to use as money. They were light enough to carry on journeys. They did not require weighing by **merchants** because of their seals. During the 400s BC, stamped coins gradually replaced **ingots** across the Mediterranean region and the **Middle East**. The ancient empires of Persia, Greece, and Rome created money systems using coins.

What did ancient coins look like?

Ancient coins were usually round. They were made from the metals found in the local area. Most were stamped with a symbol of the government leader or the place they were made.

Odd-shaped coins

Can you imagine carrying coins shaped like knives in your pocket? The ancient Chinese made coins in the shape of tools (knives, spades, and hoes) and shells. Some ancient Olbian (Russian) coins were shaped like dolphins (see photo above). The earliest Roman coins were rectangular pieces of bronze.

Early minting methods

The earliest coins were **minted** (made from metal) individually by hand. To simplify and speed up the process, ancient minters developed **moulds**, or casts. With casts, many coins of the same weight could be made at once.

The melted metal was poured into the casts. Once removed from the cast, the coins were hammered on each side with a metal stamp, or die, to imprint them with official government seal. Although coins in modern times are made by machine, the basic method of using casts and dies remains the same.

This iron die was used to stamp English coins around AD 1070. When pressed against a blank coin and struck with a hammer, the die left the imprint of William I's face on the coin's surface.

The face of a leader

The Romans were the first to stamp the image of a living person on a coin. After winning in war, Julius Caesar featured his portrait on a coin in 44 BC.

Solve it!

When Alexander the Great took control of the Persian Empire, he captured large amounts of gold. He brought much of the gold back to Greece. After this, the value of gold decreased in Greece. Why?

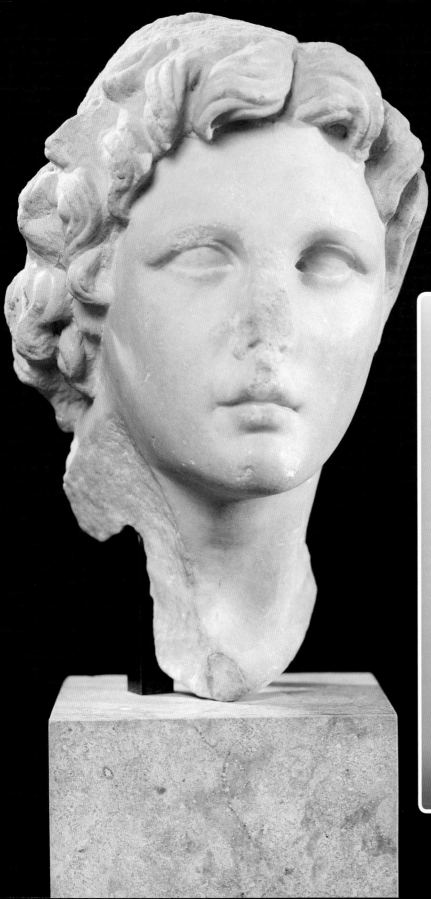

Alexander the Great

Alexander the Great became king of Macedonia (an area in modern Greece) 336 BC. Through war and **conquest**, he created a large kingdom that stretched from the Mediterranean Sea to India.

Alexander paid his soldiers in cash. This practice spread coins throughout his empire. Alexander the Great significantly increased the use of coins as money in the ancient world.

Who invented paper money?

China is credited with many early inventions, including the invention of paper money. From 200 BC onwards, the Chinese made round coins that had holes in the middle. Travelling **merchants** placed these coins on strings and wore them around their necks. The merchants found the strings of coins heavy and inconvenient to carry.

The first banknotes

Around AD 700, merchants started depositing their coins with bankers. The bankers would print paper notes in return. These paper notes were equal in value to the amount of coins deposited. The merchants could take the paper notes to the bank in their home town and receive the money from the bank.

Government paper money

In approximately AD 1020, the government of the Song Dynasty in China began printing paper money. The **seal** of both the emperor and the emperor's **treasurer** was printed on each banknote. Since the government was strong, it **guaranteed** the banknotes were worth the value printed on them. People grew to trust the paper money because it could be used to make purchases in the same way coins had been used.

These Chinese banknotes were printed by the Ming Dynasty around AD 1375. The paper was made from the bark of a mulberry tree.

Marco Polo

Marco Polo was an Italian merchant who travelled across Asia for 24 years. When he returned home in 1295, Polo brought news of Chinese inventions, including paper money.

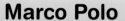

Flying money

The earliest Chinese paper money was called "flying money" or "flying cash" because the banknotes could fly away in a strong wind.

When did paper money appear in other countries?

Europeans heard about paper money through the reports of Marco Polo in the 1200s. However, they did not use paper money until the mid-1600s. In the **Middle Ages**, Europe was made up of many small kingdoms that were frequently at war with one another. People did not have confidence in their governments. As a result, they would not have confidence in paper money printed by those governments.

Handwritten notes

In the late 1200s, bankers and **merchants** in northern Italy began to use handwritten documents as money. Special signed papers, called bills of exchange, allowed merchants to travel and trade in distant countries without having to carry coins.

The first printed banknotes in Europe

In 1661, Sweden became the first European country to use printed money. During a **shortage** of coins, the Swedish Stockholm Bank began to issue banknotes. During the next 200 years, other European governments experimented with paper money. This usually occurred when supplies of metal were low, especially during wars.

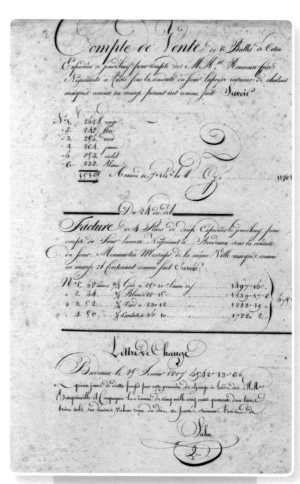

This European bill of exchange was a written order to pay a certain amount of money from the bank account of one trader to another trader's account.

John Law

Born in Scotland, John Law (1671–1729) studied **economics**. He had many new ideas about money. He thought his country should establish, or start, a national bank and use paper banknotes. Scotland rejected his ideas, so Law moved to France. There, he helped establish paper banknotes as formal **currency** in 1716.

Banknotes in Asia

The Japanese began using paper money during the 1600s. At first, most Japanese banknotes were issued privately by **Shinto** priests. At that time, Shinto temples acted like banks. Since people trusted the priests, they also trusted the paper money to work as well as coins. Later, paper money was issued by **feudal clans**. A central Japanese government began printing paper money in the late 1800s.

Banknotes in the Americas

Paper money helped spark the **American war of Independence**. In the 1700s, many local banks printed paper money in the 13 British **colonies** in America. The government in Great Britain did not approve of these banknotes. The government punished colonial businesses for using them. Many colonists grew angry at this decision and supported independence from Great Britain.

In the 1700s, paper banknotes in Japan were made to look like bookmarks.

Going back to coins

China had already returned to using coin currency by the time paper money started appearing in other countries. By the 1400s, China had issued so much paper money that the banknotes lost their value. China returned to coin currency by 1455 and did not use paper money again until the early 1900s.

Playing cards as money?

French Canada used unusual paper money in 1685. Because of a shortage of coins, the government paid their soldiers with playing cards. The playing cards were marked with a value on the back. The cards could be used to buy goods and services.

What money was used during the Age of Exploration?

By the early 1500s, long ocean voyages were possible due to improvements in sailing ships. Over the next 200 years, Europeans sailed to Asia, Africa, and the Americas to create new travel routes. This period of time was called the Age of Exploration. As sailing routes were mapped, trade between countries increased. Some countries still used **bartering** to exchange goods. However, coins were also frequently used to buy goods such as sugar, spices, rice, and cotton.

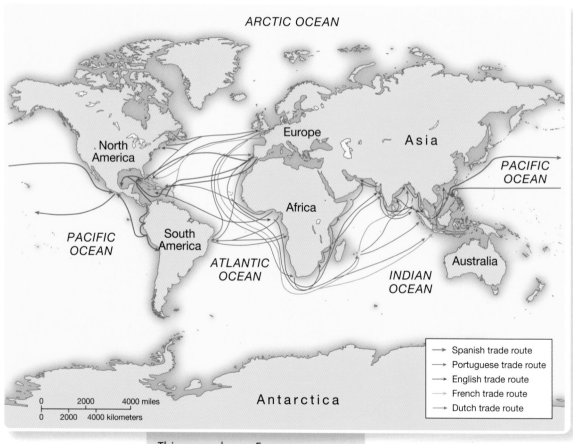

This map shows European trading routes during the 1700s.

These Spanish 50-reales coins were made in 1618. All silver coins minted in Spain around this time, including the more common Spanish dollar, displayed the same designs as those shown here.

The Spanish dollar

Spanish explorers discovered rich supplies of gold and silver in the Americas. Soon, Spain became the most powerful country in the world. Millions of Spanish silver coins, called "Spanish dollars", were used all over the world. Many other countries decided to adopt, or start using, the Spanish dollar as their own government's money. Each country cut or stamped the coins differently to show its government's **seal**.

Until 1850, the Spanish dollar was the most widely used coin in the world. Many modern day **currencies** were originally based on the Spanish dollar. These include the Canadian dollar, the US dollar, the Chinese yuan, the Philippine peso, and currencies throughout Central and South America.

Pieces of eight

During much of the 1600s and 1700s, the Spanish dollar was the unofficial currency of the British **colonies** in North America. So that people could give change, the dollar was actually cut into eight pieces. So, another name for the Spanish dollar became "pieces of eight".

Spanish dollars in South Africa

The tip of South Africa, called the Cape of Good Hope, became a resting point for explorers and traders travelling between Europe and Asia. In the 1650s, the South Africans began **minting** Spanish dollars. They stamped varied designs on the dollars. This practice enabled the South Africans to trade with many different countries.

However, using many foreign currencies became confusing. To clear the confusion, the South African government introduced the Cape Rix Daller. This currency made it possible to compare the values of Spanish dollars from different countries. The South Africans could then make accurate exchanges with foreign traders.

Solve it!

Spanish dollars could be cut into eight pieces. A merchant used three Spanish dollars to pay for several bags of sugar. The sugar cost 2 and 3/8 Spanish dollars. How much money did the **merchant** receive in change?

In Australia in the early 1800s, British settlers did not have a large supply of coins. Instead of making new coins, the British government sent Spanish dollars for the settlers to use. The government cut holes in the centre and stamped a new design on the metal to show that the coins were now British money.

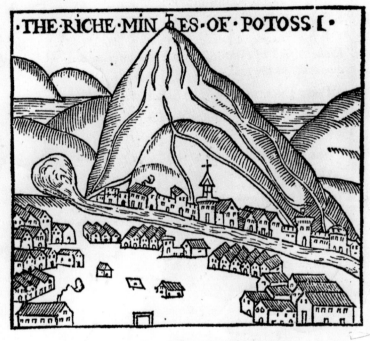

THE
DISCOVERIE AND CONQVEST
of the Prouinces of *PERV*, and
the *Nauigation* in the South
Sea, along that Coast.
And also of the ritche *Mines*
of *POTOSI*.

·THE·RICHE·MINES·OF·POTOSSI·

❡ *Imprinted at London* by Richard Ihones. *Febru. 6. 1581.*

This advertisement, printed in 1581, promoted the riches that could be found in the silver mines of Bolivia. Unfortunately, many native people died working in the mines because of the dangerous conditions.

The Spanish mints of South America

In the early 1500s, large deposits of silver were discovered in Mexico and South America by Spanish explorers. The Spanish built many mines to remove the silver from the earth. They also built mints to produce the Spanish dollars within the colonies of Spain. Beginning in 1536, Spanish dollars were minted in Mexico City and areas of South America that became Peru, Bolivia, and Columbia.

How did modern countries develop their money?

The money used by modern governments tells a story about that country's history. Some countries developed their money based on coins introduced during worldwide trade. Others were forced to adopt, or start using, the money of a nation that controlled them. War, power, and trade have influenced modern money around the world.

Colonies in North America

France, England, Holland, and Spain established **colonies** in North America during the 1600s. Coins from each of these nations could be used to purchase goods. After declaring independence from Great Britain in 1776, each of the 13 new states of the United States began to make its own coins and banknotes. With 13 different **currencies** plus foreign coins in use, trading became confusing.

The United States dollar

After the US Constitution was approved in 1790, the new United States government agreed on one common money system. This new system relied on the dollar as the basic unit, which could be divided into 100 cents.

Initially, coins were made of gold, silver, and copper. Since 1965, US coins have been created using mainly copper and nickel. Paper banknotes (or "**bills**" as they are called in the US) were introduced widely in 1861 to help pay for the Civil War. These notes gained the nickname "greenbacks" because of the colour of the ink on the back of the notes.

Each type of US coin or banknote shows the face of a famous American leader. George Washington appears on the quarter (shown below). The face of Benjamin Franklin appears on the $100 bill (banknote).

Dirty money

Beware! Paper banknotes are not clean! A 2002 study in the United States showed disease-causing germs on 94 per cent of the notes tested.

Money in Kenya (East Africa)

Official currency began circulation in Kenya in the early 1800s. Before that time, people in Kenya **bartered** to get and sell goods. From 1800–1850, European **merchants** used silver **thalers** to conduct business in Kenya. People who lived along the Kenyan coast frequently used the thalers to buy goods and services.

Beginning in 1895, workers from India built an important railway in Kenya. These workers were paid in Indian rupees. For a time, the rupee became the official currency of the Kenya-Uganda region.

In 1922, the East African shilling was introduced as the official currency of Kenya, Uganda, and Tanganyika (now part of Tanzania). The East African shilling was equivalent to the currency being using in Great Britain. Kenya was a British colony at that time.

Kenyan shilling

Kenya became an independent nation in 1964. The new country began printing its own money two years later. Since that time, Kenyan coins and banknotes have been printed in different amounts of shillings and cents. In Kenya, one shilling is equal to 100 cents.

Old and new

The modern country of Turkey exists where the first coins were made around 640 BC. Turkey now has one of the most recently adopted currencies. The new Turkish Lira was introduced in 2005.

A portrait of Kenya's first president appears on all Kenyan banknotes and coins. Mzee Jomo Kenyatta served as president from 1964 to 1973 and is considered to be the founding father of the Kenyan nation.

Banknotes and coins in Venezuela are very colorful. The newest banknotes, printed in 2008, contain ink colors never before used in Venezuela.

Money in Venezuela (South America)

From the 1500s, Spain established colonies in Venezuela. As a result, the Spanish dollar was used as its currency for about 300 years. In 1821, Venezuela won its independence from Spain. The new country adopted the money of its neighbour, Colombia. The basic currency unit, the peso, was developed from the Spanish dollar.

In 1848, Venezuela switched its currency to the franco, or French franc. Then Venezuela tried to create its own unique currency in 1854. The basic unit, the venezolano, did not last long.

In 1879, the Venezuelan government adopted the bolivar as its official currency. The bolivar was divided into 100 centimos. The first bolivar banknotes were printed in 1940.

The latest change in Venezuelan currency occurred in 2008. The government adopted the bolivar fuerte as the basic unit of money. The new name means "strong bolivar".

The pound sterling

Unlike most other nations, England has maintained the same currency since around AD 928, when the national currency was established. As then, the official currency of the United Kingdom today is the pound sterling, commonly called the "pound". Today, the pound is divided into 100 pence.

Pre-decimal pound

Before **decimalization** in 1971, giving change for the pound was quite complicated! Instead of being easily divided by 10 or 100, the pound was divided into 20 shillings. Each shilling equalled 12 pence. That's 240 pence to the pound!

What money is used around the world today?

Over 170 different **currencies** are used around the world. Most countries have their own currency, but some neighbouring nations share money. Shared currencies exist in Europe, Africa, and the Caribbean.

Coins and banknotes

Most currencies today exist in both coins and banknotes. Typically, modern coins are made from mixtures of inexpensive metals. The coins have value because they are stamped and **guaranteed** by the government. The same is true for paper money. The paper itself is not expensive. But the banknotes are worth the amount printed on them by that country's government.

This Japanese 500 yen banknote has a watermark incorporated into its paper. A watermark is a special picture or pattern that can be seen only when the note is held up to light.

Queen Elizabeth II

The UK's Queen Elizabeth II (1926–) holds an unusual record. Her portrait has appeared on the currency of more than 30 different countries—more than that of any individual. Many former British **colonies** joined the **Commonwealth of Nations** after gaining independence. Sixteen of these nations still consider Queen Elizabeth II as their chief public representative, or "head of state".

Shh! It's a secret!

The process of making banknotes is secret and complicated. Well-trained artists use special designs, paper, and ink. Most banknotes include features to prevent people from making fake money. Some countries use inks that only show up in ultraviolet light. Other inks cannot be photocopied. Most banknotes have a watermark design worked into the paper. Many banknotes also contain security threads made of plastic or metal foil.

Similarities in currency

Several former colonies of Spain use money called pesos. Peso was the name given to the Spanish dollar in the 1600s when it spread throughout Central and South America. Peso means "weight" in the Spanish language. Today, the countries of Mexico, the Philippines, Chile, Cuba, Uruguay, Colombia, and Argentina use versions of the peso.

Money around the world

Country	Currency
Brazil	Real
China	Yuan
Denmark	Danish Krone
Ecuador	US Dollar
Egypt	Egyptian Pound
France	Euro
Germany	Euro
India	Indian Rupee
Japan	Yen
Kenya	Kenyan Shilling
Mexico	Mexican New Peso
Nigeria	Naira
Philippines	Philippine Peso
Saudi Arabia	Saudi Riyal
South Africa	Rand
Spain	Euro
Thailand	Baht
United Kingdom	Pound Sterling
United States	US Dollar

Solve it!

Currency from one country can be exchanged for currency from another country. An exchange rate is used to determine the value of one type of money compared to another. For example, one Australian dollar might be worth 4.9 Danish kroner on a particular day. If someone from Australia wanted to exchange 100 Australian dollars on that day, how many Danish kroner could she get in return?

Groovy!

Most modern coins have a grooved edge. In the past, dishonest traders filed down the smooth edges of coins to steal some of the precious metal.

Most coins today are made from inexpensive metals such as copper and nickel.

Shared currency in Europe

In 1993, many countries in Europe joined together to form the European Union (EU). Members of the EU agree to follow a common set of laws about trade, agriculture, and business development. Some members of the EU also share a common currency, the euro. Currently, 16 EU member states use the euro as their only currency. Together, these 16 countries are called the "eurozone".

Countries that use the euro as their only currency are shown in green on the map. Together, these countries are called the "eurozone".

Iceland

Finland

Sweden

Norway

Estonia

Latvia

Lithuania

Denmark

Ireland

Netherlands

U.K.

Poland

Belgium

Germany

Luxembourg

Czech Republic

Slovakia

Austria

Hungary

Switzerland

Romania

France

Slovenia

Bulgaria

Italy

Portugal

Spain

Greece

Cyprus

Malta

zone

EU members not using

Not EU members

| 0 | 200 | 400 miles |
| 0 | 200 | 400 kilometers |

Weighing the pros and cons

To decide whether to adopt the euro, many countries have weighed the possible positive and negative outcomes of sharing currency with other nations.

Possible positive outcomes:

1. Large savings of money from not having to exchange currencies.

2. Eurozone is stronger than one individual country.

3. Easier to trade and do business.

4. Prices for goods stay low and stable.

5. Lower rates for borrowing money.

Possible negative outcomes:

1. Cannot change money laws for your own country if needed.

2. May have to "bail out" other member countries to keep euro strong.

Crisis in Greece

In early 2010, the Greek government announced that it did not have enough money to run the country or to pay back many people who had lent the country money. The EU and a multinational organization called the International Monetary Fund, or IMF, decided to let Greece borrow an enormous amount of euros to help. In return, Greece must try to reduce the amount of money it spends and find ways to help its economy grow. The borrowed money must eventually be paid back.

What other forms of money exist?

Money does not exist only as coins and banknotes. Today, several forms of cashless money are used to buy goods and services.

Computer files

Money can exist as an electronic file on a computer. Many people have their earnings added to their bank accounts electronically. Their bills can then be paid online. Money can be moved electronically from one bank to another. All of these transactions happen through special communication systems used by computers.

Debit cards, credit cards

Today, money can also exist in the form of a plastic card. These plastic cards have a magnetic strip, which holds a customer's information. A debit card is linked to a person's bank account. The person can use the debit card to buy food or other goods. The shop's computer reads the card's magnetic strip and sends an electronic message to the person's bank. The bank transfers, or sends, money electronically from the person's account to the shop.

People can also borrow money to pay for things. A bank or business, called a credit card company, agrees to an amount a person can borrow. The credit card company gives the person a credit card. When the credit card is used, the shop's computer communicates with the credit card company. The card company sends electronic money to the shop. The person must pay back the credit company at a later time. Credit card companies charge high fees (interest) for the opportunity to pay the money back over time, instead of all at once.

Many banks and shops have cashpoint machines for their customers to use. A person uses a plastic card linked to his or her bank account to withdraw money.

How can you make your own coin collection?

Coin collecting is one of the most popular hobbies in the world! Some people collect coins to learn about the historical events, places, and people shown on the coins. Others view coins as works of art. Some people collect coins as an investment. They believe their coins will be worth more money in the future.

People collect different coins according to personal interest. Some collectors try to get a coin from every country. Others prefer coins from the history of one particular country. Some people collect coins that show similar pictures, such as ships, horses, or trees.

How to organize coins

Hard plastic trays work well for storing coins. Only one coin should be placed in each space. Small paper envelopes can also be used. Special details about each coin can be written on the paper envelopes or in a separate notebook.

Fun hobby, fancy name

Studying and collecting **currency** has a formal name— **numismatics**. Originally, numismatics related to coins only. Now, the term includes studying and collecting paper money, too.

What not to do with coins

Coins will **corrode** over time if they are not treated carefully. Never use metal polish or a wire brush to clean coins. This will cause the designs to wear away. Also, do not store coins in bendable plastic envelopes. In time, the envelopes will become sticky and will ruin the coins.

This collector has organized one type of coin, the United States quarter, by the year each was **minted**. Other collectors might group coins by country ,or by type of design.

Timeline

Before 10,000 BC	People begin trading goods.
8000 BC	People start raising crops and animals on farms.
6000 BC	Cows are used as the first form of money.
1850 BC	In Mesopotamia, ingots are used as money.
1750 BC	Code of Hammurabi gives laws about the use of money.
1400 BC	In China, cowrie shells are used as money.
640 BC	First coins are made and used in Lydia.
300s BC	Alexander the Great spreads Greek coins from India to Egypt.
AD 1020	First paper money is printed in China.
1295	Marco Polo brings word of Chinese paper money to Italy.
1500s	Spanish dollar becomes most widely used coin in the world.
1661	Sweden prints the first paper banknote in Europe.
1792	Dollar becomes the official currency of the United States.
1988	Australia introduces the first set of plastic banknotes.
2002	Euro coins and banknotes are introduced in the European Union.

Answers to Solve it!

Page 7
100 feathers

Page 16
The value of a precious metal is related to how easy or difficult it is to find. When the Greeks had a surplus of gold, the gold was no longer as valuable as when it was in short supply.

Page 26
5/8 Spanish dollars

Page 37
100 x 4.9 = 490 Danish kroner

Glossary

American War of Independence war that took place between 1775 and 1783 during which the American colonies won independence from British rule, taxation and political control

bill term used in the US and other places for a banknote

barter exchange of goods or services without using money

colony settlement in one country that is formed and ruled by another country

Commonwealth of Nations organization of 54 members, most of which used to be part of the British Empire

conquest act of taking over other lands, as was done during early wars

corrode wear away over time

currency money (both banknotes and coins) that is used to purchase goods and services

decimalization act of changing to a decimal system based on units of 10

economics study of the production and use of goods and services

feudal clans Japanese family groups who defended their land through war

guarantee take responsibility for; promise

ingot piece of metal shaped in a mould

merchant person who trades goods

Middle Ages time period in European history from AD 400 to about 1500

Middle East term used to refer to countries stretching from Turkey to Northern Africa, and across Iran, including Egypt, Israel, Iraq, Saudi Arabia, Libya and others

mint produce money by stamping metal

mould hollow container used to give shape to hot or liqud material, such as wax or metal, when it cools and hardens

numismatics studying and collecting currency

seal special design stamped on wax, paper, or metal

Shinto a religion native to Japan in which nature and ancestors are honored

shortage less than what is needed

surplus more than what is needed

symbol ancient Greek gold or silver coin

stater ancient Greek gold or silver coin

thaler silver coin that was used as currency in Europe

treasurer person appointed to manage the finances of a country, company, or other organization

Find out more

Books

*Coins and Other Currency: A Kid's Guide to Coin Collecting (*Money Matters: A Kid's Guide to Money*)* Tamra Orr (Mitchell Lane Publishers, 2008)

Graphing Money (Real World Data) Patrick Catel (Heinemann Library, 2009)

Money (Earning, Saving, Spending), Barbara Hall, (Heinemann Library, 2011)

The World Encyclopedia of Coins & Coin Collecting, Dr James Mackay (Lorenz Books, 2010)

Websites

http://www.banknotes.com/images.htm
Do you wonder what banknotes from Antarctica look like? The World Currency Gallery shows pictures of banknotes from countries throughout the world.

www.ehow.co.uk/about_5038400_coin-collecting-supplies-kids.html
Tells you more about coin collecting and explains what you might need to get started on your own collection.

http://www.royalmint.com/
Learn about the history of the UK Royal Mint. Did you know that the Mint has been located in many different places over the centures and that is now in Wales? You can also find out details of the Mint's collections and current exhibitions.

Places to visit

Most local and national museums have coin collections. Your local museum may even have ancient coins that have been found in your area.

Index